Applebet

A is for Annie · · And so is this Book

Applebet
AN ABC

CLYDE WATSON

Pictures by Wendy Watson

A Sunburst Book

Farrar, Straus and Giroux

A is for **apple** as everyone knows
Can you follow this one wherever it goes?

B is for **Bet** in the top of the tree
Who picked it & shined it & gave it to me

C is for **cart** standing ready below
Brimful of apples & ready to go

Soft C is for **cider** made first thing today
We'll keep a jug handy to drink on the way

CH is for **Cherry**, the little red mare
Giddy-up, Cherry—we're off to the fair!

D is for **daisies** alongside the lane
Here I go, weaving a long daisy chain

E is for **egg woman** trotting to town
With a basket of eggs all speckled & brown

F is for **farmer** at work on the land
He stops for a moment & waves his hand

G is for **gossips** who lean on the gate
Wagging their tongues at a terrible rate

Soft G is for **gentleman** dressed to a tee
Riding by in a carriage, silk hat on his knee

H is for **hay wagon** going so fast
That it upsets the apple cart as it roars past

I is for **innkeeper** playing at dice
Cheer up! he shouts. You'll be there in a trice!

J is for **juggler**, & well may you stare
At the way he makes oranges dance in midair

K is for **kites** of all colors—Come buy!
Pick a bird or a bat or a dragon to fly!

L is for **lollipop**, licorice or lime,
Root beer or peppermint, two for a dime

M is for **magic** — Hey, what's that?
A rabbit pulled out of an empty hat!

N is for **nap** in the shade at noon
A nap that's over all too soon

O is for **oink**, an ominous sound
Wake up, my darling, there's trouble around!

P is for **pig** escaped from his pen
And he's eating our apples up, eight nine ten!

QU is for **quarrel** about pigs on the loose
With shouting & stamping & no sign of truce

R is for **rain** falling out of the blue—
I'm going inside, won't you come too?

S is for **sausages**, spicy & sweet
Hot off the spit & ready to eat

SH is for **sh-h!** Please, ladies & gents!
This way for the puppet show—tickets, five cents!

T is for **table** set up for the judge
With pumpkins & cabbages, jellies & fudge

TH is for **thief** with his eye on the goods
He sweeps up an armful & heads for the woods

U is for **uproar** — Ah! Down you go!
So much for thieves, now on with the show

V is for **velvet**, green, blue & red
A rainbow of ribbons strung up on a thread

W is for **winner** who takes the prize
For best of the lot, be it pickles or pies

WH is for **whisper** in somebody's ear
Oh say it again, for I couldn't quite hear

X is for **X-mark** carved on a tree

And it stands for a kiss to you from me

Y is for **yes**, it's time to go
The stars are out & the road is slow

Z is for **zigzag** all the way back
Home again, home again, appledy-jack